SEVEN DIMENSIONS OF GOD'S GRACE

Keys to Meeting All Your Needs
And to Live in Freedom

ABRAHAM JOHN

7 Dimensions of the Grace of God

The Key to Meeting all your Needs and Live in Freedom

Copyright © 2015 by Abraham John

ISBN: 978-1-948330-28-2

All rights reserved. No part of this book may be reproduced or transmitted in any form or by any means, electronic or mechanical—including photocopying, recording, or by any information storage and retrieval system without permission in writing from the author. Please direct inquiries to mim@maximpact.org.

Unless otherwise noted, all Scripture taken from the New King James Version®. Copyright © 1982 by Thomas Nelson. Used by permission. All rights reserved.

Scriptures marked KJV are taken from the King James Version of the Bible. Public Domain in the USA.

Scriptures marked Philips are taken from The New Testament in Modern English by J.B Philips copyright © 1960, 1972 J. B. Phillips. Administered by The Archbishops' Council of the Church of England. Used by Permission.

Contents

Preface	5
Introduction	11
Chapter 1: The Law and Grace	15
Chapter 2: The Benefits of Grace	47
Chapter 3: 7 Dimensions of God's Grace	61
Chapter 4: Three Levels of Grace	79
More Books & Resources	89

Preface

Grace is an overused word in the Body of Christ just like love, glory, and praise the Lord. When people talk about the grace of God, they usually mean His mercy, forgiveness, or they might mean the famous definition of "unmerited favor." However, that's not all there is to grace.

Grace has many more implications, meanings, and benefits attached to it. My attempt here, is to explore the depths of the grace of God, so that you can receive from Him all that has been made available to us.

The grace God has made available to each one of us, is similar to someone making a billion dollar deposit into your account, and you never realizing it. In that person's eyes you are a very rich person, but those riches are not benefitting you because of your unawareness.

In God's eyes you are saved, blessed, anointed, delivered, rich, and more than a conqueror. However, most people's lives do not resemble this because they lack the revelation of the grace of God.

This study will give you the key to the solutions for many of the problems you are facing in your life. The grace of God contains all the solutions you need for life's situations. Whether it is emotional, spiritual, financial, social, or problems in our family, there is nothing that the grace of God cannot solve. This is the teaching you have been waiting for all your life!

We can either receive what we need from God through His grace; or, we can depend on our ability, strength, or works. When we depend on our works there will always be a struggle for everything. There will be never enough—not enough energy, much effort but few results, too much toil and sweat but not much harvest.

When you receive a revelation of the grace of God there will always be plenty. Things will be easier because you will be in rest, as God will be working on your behalf. In fact, the grace of God will be working for you.

The best example I can think of, is someone trying to reach California on the west-coast from New York on the east-coast using a horse and buggy, compared to flying in an airplane. Which one is easier, traveling in a horse and buggy or flying in an airplane? Which one would you prefer using in this day and age?

Trying to do things without God's grace is like traveling in a horse and buggy. When you operate in the grace of God, what you could not accomplish in twenty years with your efforts, the grace of God will do in one year.

Now the question is: What is the grace of God?

There is so much misinformation and wrong teaching throughout the Body of Christ about grace these days. Many people interchange *grace* with the word *excuse*. God never meant to excuse when He decided to show His grace toward us. Neither is it a license to live in sin or to remain the same. Those are totally opposite of the true grace of God.

Remember the stories of the woman who was caught in adultery, and the Samaritan woman. They did not go back to sin. They were transformed when they had an encounter with the grace of God.

No one ever had an encounter with the grace of God and remained the same, or had a tendency to live in sin or even to do any type of sin. Grace is a spiritual law like any other law that God established. When you understand and apply it to your life and circumstances, you will experience the benefit of it.

Definition of God's grace: Grace is the combination of God's love, favor, compassion, kindness, mercy, forgiveness, blessings, and power freely bestowed upon us to meet our needs that we cannot meet in our own strength.

Everything in this universe works according to laws established by God. The Old Testament laws could not accomplish in us what God wanted, so He decided to introduce another law called grace. When I say that grace is a law, I don't mean the Old Testament types of laws that we are familiar with. I am talking about laws like gravity, the law of the spirit of life, etc.

> Romans 8:3, For what the **law could not do** in that it was weak through the flesh, God *did* by sending His own Son in the likeness of sinful flesh, on account of sin: He condemned sin in the flesh.

In my study of the Bible, I have found that there are different kinds of grace mentioned in the New Testament. The word *grace* appears 145 times in the New King James Version. Out of those, 125 are in the New Testament. Thank God we are living in the age of grace!

There are two key verses I want to use as the foundation of our study, and both are taken from the gospel of John:

> John 1:14, And the Word became flesh and dwelt among us, and we beheld His glory, the glory as of the only begotten of the Father, **full of grace and truth**.

> John 1:16, And of His fullness **we have all received, and grace for grace.**

Those are two very powerful Bible verses. Jesus was full of grace and truth. If you look at Jesus, you will see what grace looks like, because He was full of it all the time. Grace overflowed from His life. He never ran short or lacked grace. Out of His fullness we have all received grace for grace.

I want to explain what is meant by Jesus being full of grace. I hope you recall what grace means. It is His love, favor, compassion, mercy, kindness, forgiveness, blessings and power—all combined to help a person. Wow!

Can you imagine that God looks at a person and is willing to help that individual with His love, compassion, mercy, kindness, forgiveness, blessings, and power? What would happen to that person?

Do you think they will go back the same way they came? I don't think so. They will go back filled and with every need met. This is why Jesus says, "Be thou made whole" when He sets a person free. To be made whole means that nothing is missing, nothing is lacking, and nothing is broken. This is the way God fixes a person or situation.

The reason why we don't receive such blessings these days is because we don't understand what the grace of God means. This is why God helped me to prepare this study; so that you can be made whole. There won't be another day in your life that you are struggling to meet your needs, or saying, "Oh, maybe God does not want me to have it." No. That season is over.

Introduction

Since the fall of mankind, in each age God began to deal with us differently. The ways that God dealt with mankind in each age is called a *dispensation*. A dispensation is a period of time in which God deals with mankind based on a particular covenant, promise, or principle.

From the creation of Adam until now there have been six dispensations or covenants—meaning six different ways that God related to mankind. There is one more dispensation yet to be fulfilled. It will begin after the second coming of Christ.

This study is not about dispensations. Nevertheless, I want to cover these briefly so you can know what they are, and what dispensation we are living in right now.

When one dispensation is completed and a new one is introduced, the old one becomes invalid. God does not require us to keep the terms and conditions of the old when He begins to deal with humanity based on a new dispensation (covenant).

Only the promises and benefits from previous dispensations continue on to the next one—not the rules (terms and conditions). This is very important to understand; otherwise, it will create a lot of confusion in your walk with God.

To simplify it, God is not dealing with us now as He dealt with Noah or Moses. Thank God!

We are in the best dispensation God has dealt with mankind since the fall. Everyone since the fall desired to see and live in the day we are now living in. It is unfortunate that many look back to the Old Testament and wish they lived then.

THE SEVEN DISPENSATIONS ARE THE FOLLOWING:

1. Dispensation of Innocence

This period began with the creation of Adam, and ended when he sinned.

2. Dispensation of Conscience

After the fall, mankind lived for a while based on his conscience, which lasted until the time of Noah.

3. Dispensation of Human Government

Mankind began to make his own rules and establish kingdoms on this earth. This lasted from Noah until the time of Abraham.

4. Dispensation of Promise

From the time of Abraham, God began to deal with man based on the promise He made with Abraham and this lasted until the law was introduced through Moses.

5. Dispensation of Law

God made a covenant with the people of Israel and gave them His Law, which is called the Old Testament or Old Covenant. This lasted until John the Baptist.

6. Dispensation of Grace

God began to deal with mankind based on His love and grace, and not based on man's performance. this began with the birth of Jesus, and will go on until Jesus' second coming.

7. Dispensation of the Millennial Reign

This will begin when Christ comes to set up His kingdom on this earth, and we will reign with Him for a thousand years.

We are now living in the dispensation or age of grace. This means God decided to show His favor, or grace (acceptance) to anyone who will respond to His love demonstrated to us through giving us His only Son.

Whoever believes in His Son Jesus, God will accept, forgive their sins, and make them His children. No other condition is involved, nothing whatsoever.

He does not deal with us based on the Old Testament laws, because we are not living during that former time period right now. We will see this in more detail in the following pages.

> Ephesians 3:2, If indeed you have heard of the **dispensation of the grace of God** which was given to me for you.

Now, let us look at the seven dimensions of the grace of God that was revealed through Jesus Christ to meet all our needs.

CHAPTER 1

The Law and Grace

Since the fall, God's relationship with mankind and mankind's relationship with God has changed dramatically. God, Himself, did not change neither did His love for us. However, our capacity to understand changed from age to age.

We are now living in a world that is deteriorating daily because of sin. Though outwardly it looks like we are making progress, in many ways life is not any better now than it was a thousand years ago. We have more conveniences, luxuries, and technology, but there are more sicknesses, and people are lonelier and more unhappy in general.

Jesus came to preach the acceptable year of the Lord. Though it says a *year*, this does not mean a literal year, but rather represents an age.

Luke 4:18-19, The Spirit of the Lord *is* upon Me, because He has anointed Me to preach the gospel to *the* poor; He has sent Me to heal the brokenhearted, to proclaim liberty to *the* captives and recovery of sight to *the* blind, *to* set at liberty those who are oppressed; **to proclaim the acceptable year of the Lord**.

Following Christ or seeking the kingdom of God is not obeying a bunch of rules and regulations. Rather, it is a relationship with the King of kings and the Lord of lords.

Are too many people have reduced Christianity to simple a bunch of rules. This is far from the truth. We are going to see how we fulfill every commandment in the Bible by having a relationship with Jesus Christ and with one another.

How Does a Believer in Christ Fulfill the Requirements of the Law or the Ten Commandments?

The Ten Commandments were given as part of the law. In fact, these merely served as the introduction to the rest of the law. So, when Moses started writing what God was speaking and gave to him, he started with the Ten Commandments.

There was a big fight going on in America concerning the Ten Commandments. The government wanted to remove them from public places, while some people in the church think the country is going to go downhill because these are being removed.

Do you still want to fulfill the Ten Commandments?

Read the following verses, and do what they say. No nation or person will go under if they practice the following two verses from the Bible. You will fulfill the whole law if you only obey the following two verses:

> Romans 13:8-10, Owe no one anything except to love one another, for he who loves another has fulfilled the law. For the commandments, 'You shall not commit adultery,' 'You shall not murder,' 'You shall not steal,' 'You shall not bear false witness,' 'You shall not covet,' and if *there is* any other commandment, are *all* summed up in this saying, namely, 'You shall love your neighbor as yourself.' Love does no harm to a neighbor; **therefore love is the fulfillment of the law**.

We do not fulfill the law by keeping rules, observing certain rituals, following spiritual disciplines, adopting a certain dress code, or focusing on outward appearance. We fulfill the law by doing the following.

> Galatians 5:13-15, For you, brethren, have been called to liberty; only do not *use* liberty as an opportunity for the flesh, but through

love serve one another. **For all the law is fulfilled in one word**, *even* in this: 'You shall love your neighbor as yourself.' But if you bite and devour one another, beware lest you be consumed by one another!

Many believers are traveling in two boats, with one foot in the law and the other foot on grace. As a result, they are not going anywhere and they are not sure which one is which.

This comes about mainly because they fear losing their salvation. The second reason why this occurs, is because most had no foundational teaching about the Christian faith. The third reason is most do not know what it means when the Bible uses the word *love*.

Most of us were never loved unconditionally by anyone, so we do not know how to receive the love of God nor how to express it to others. The only love many of us know is the love between a man and a woman, which often is mostly lustful. The Bible says the love of God is beyond our comprehension (Ephesians 3:19).

We all received a little bit of this and that from somewhere, but never gained a systematic teaching about the doctrines of the New Covenant.

As a result, people willy-nilly take Scriptures from the law and mix those with the Scriptures from the New Testament and all they get is spiritual constipation. Most people end up living a life of a crazy mash-up of both law and grace.

Four times in the epistles, Paul said that God will judge the hearts of men based on *his gospel*, and not according to the law or Ten Commandments:

> Romans 2:16, In the day when God will judge the secrets of men by Jesus Christ, according to **my gospel**.
>
> Romans 16:25, Now to Him who is able to establish you according to **my gospel** and the preaching of Jesus Christ, according to the revelation of the mystery kept secret since the world began.
>
> 1 Timothy 1:11, According to the glorious gospel of the blessed God which was committed to **my trust**.
>
> 2 Timothy 2:8, Remember that Jesus Christ, of the seed of David, was raised from the dead according to **my gospel.**

How can Paul make such bold statements? Even Jesus did not say such things. None of the authors of the four Gospels made such a statement.

Jesus came to reveal the mystery of the kingdom of God. This is what we lost because of the fall. He came to restore to us the kingdom.

I am not saying here that Paul is greater than Jesus. No way. The reason he said it is this; the mystery of God, Christ, the Church, the gospel, and the grace of God was revealed to Paul and not to anyone else—including the other apostles. How do I know this? Please read the following verses:

> Romans 16:25, Now to him that is of power to establish you according to my gospel, and the preaching of Jesus Christ, according to the revelation of the **mystery**, which was kept secret since the world began.

> Ephesians 3:2-5, If indeed you have heard of the dispensation of the grace of God which was given to me for you, how that **by revelation He made known to me the mystery** (as I have briefly written already, by which, when you read, you may understand my knowledge in the **mystery of Christ**), which in other ages was not made known to the sons of men, as it has now been revealed by the Spirit to His holy apostles and prophets.

> Ephesians 3:8-9 (KJV), Unto me, who am less than the least of all the saints, is this grace given, that I should preach among the Gentiles the **unsearchable riches of Christ**; and to make all men see what is the fellowship of the **mystery**, which from the beginning of the

world hath been hid in God, who created all things by Jesus Christ.

There is a time coming when the revelation of the grace of God will fill the whole earth. God will raise up many preachers to preach the grace of God more than anything else. They will be misunderstood and persecuted in the beginning—just as it happened in the Bible days. We need to believe and preach the gospel Paul preached. Then the end will come.

A Believer and the Works of the Law

What is the relationship between a believer in Christ and the Old Testament law? How much of it do we need to observe? Will we be judged based on the law or grace?

> Galatians 3:10-14, For as many as are of the works of the law are under the curse; for it is written, 'Cursed *is* everyone who does not continue in all things which are written in the book of the law, to do them.' But that no one is justified by the law in the sight of God *is* evident, for 'the just shall live by faith.' Yet the law is not of faith, but 'the man who does them shall live by them.'
>
> Christ has redeemed us from the curse of the law, having become a curse for us (for it is written, 'Cursed *is* everyone who hangs on a tree'), that the blessing of Abraham might

come upon the Gentiles in Christ Jesus, that we might receive the promise of the Spirit through faith.'

Nowhere in the New Testament does it say we need to keep the Old Testament laws. Instead, it says we are free from the law and its curses. If you want to remain under a curse, then just try to keep the law.

The Side Effects of Keeping the Law

When I say side effects, I mean unwanted troubles. I already mentioned one above, which is to have the curses that are mentioned in the Old Testament. That is one of the main side effects.

No one wants to be cursed or live under a curse, but many do and they do not even know it. If there is any curse operating in your life it is because you are going back to the Old Testament and trying to obey some of its rules.

There are other side effects mentioned in the New Testament, and I also want to share those with you.

It brings knowledge of sin

> Romans 3:20, Therefore by the deeds of the law no flesh will be justified in His sight, for **by the law** is **the knowledge of sin**.

> Romans 7:7, What shall we say then? *Is* the law sin? Certainly not! On the contrary, **I would not have known sin except through the law**. For I would not have known covetousness unless the law had said, 'You shall not covet.'

Those who are living under the law cannot forget their sins, nor do they feel forgiven (Hebrews 10:3). The law that is in your heart keeps reminding you of every wrong thing you ever did from childhood until now.

You will misunderstand this, thinking that it is the Holy Spirit who is reminding you. No, it's the law. The Holy Spirit will not bring to your remembrance the sins God forgave. He does not remember them at all (Hebrews 8:12; 10:17).

Consequently, most believers never go beyond the basic doctrine of Christ, which is repentance (Hebrews 5:12-6:1-2). They, like the Old Testament believers, keep repenting every year, some every week. They never go beyond that.

Since Christ died, repentance no longer means confessing our sins; it means a change of mind—changing the way we think.

It empowers sin consciousness

A believer in Christ is supposed to live by their consciousness of righteousness. As long as a person remains under the law, they will not be able to exercise consciousness of righteousness, because the law keeps reminding and empowering their sense of sin consciousness.

> Hebrews 10:1-4 For the law, having a shadow of the good things to come, *and* not the very image of the things, can never with these same sacrifices, which they offer continually year by year, make those who approach perfect. For then would they not have ceased to be offered? For the worshipers, once purified, would have had no more **consciousness of sins**. But in those *sacrifices there is* a reminder of sins every year. For *it is* not possible that the blood of bulls and goats could take away sins.

It brings wrath

> Romans 4:14-15, For if those who are of the law *are* heirs, faith is made void and the promise made of no effect, because the **law brings about wrath**; for where there is no law *there is* no transgression.

If you are under the law, you will always be afraid of God's judgment and wrath. You will live in constant fear of punishment. You will have no assurance of salvation, nor comfort of the Holy Spirit.

One of the reasons why people do not experience the benefits of grace now, is because they trust the law more than the grace of God. This means they trust in what they *do*.

In both the spirit and in the natural realms, there is a consequence whenever you break a certain law, and God is not responsible for that. Rather, that is the reason why bad things happen to good people; and they wonder why it happened to them.

Also, the law makes you angry. If you are a person who follows the law you will become angry when you see others breaking the law that you are keeping.

However, if you are under grace, when you see someone make a mistake, you will feel compassion and mercy toward them. This is why Jesus was compassionate toward sinners, while the Pharisees were angry and wanted to kill them. The law was given through Moses, but grace and truth came through Jesus Christ (John 1:17).

The law makes sin alive

Do you wonder why you cannot overcome sin though you are saved? Though by the New Birth you are dead to sin, the commandments cause sin to come alive in you. If there is no law, sin remains dead.

> Romans 7:8-11, But sin, taking opportunity by the commandment, produced in me all *manner of evil* desire. For apart from the law

sin *was* dead. I was alive once without the law, but when the commandment came, sin revived and I died. And the commandment, which *was* to *bring* life, I found to *bring* death. For sin, taking occasion by the commandment, deceived me, and by it killed *me*.

You will be under the dominion of sin

Romans 6:14, For sin shall not have dominion over you, for you are not under law but under grace.

As long as you try to keep and obey the law, you will be under the dominion of sin. This is against New Covenant theology. After Christ died and paid for our sins, sin lost its dominion; and so, no one needs to remain under its power any longer.

The law is the strength empowering sin

Do you know why you feel the tendency to sin so strongly? It is because of the laws you are trying to keep, whether consciously or subconsciously.

1 Corinthians 15:56, The sting of death *is* sin, and the **strength of sin** is **the law**.

1 Corinthians 15:56-57 (Philips), It is sin which gives death its power, and **it is the law which gives sin its strength.** All thanks to God, then,

who gives us the victory over these things through our Lord Jesus Christ!

If you keep the law, you are separated from Christ and have fallen from grace

If you keep one commandment from the law, you are obliged to keep the whole law.

> Galatians 5:3-6, And I testify again to every man who becomes circumcised that he is a debtor to keep the whole law. You have become estranged from Christ, you who *attempt to* be justified by law; **you have fallen from grace**. For we through the Spirit eagerly wait for the hope of righteousness by faith. For in Christ Jesus neither circumcision nor un-circumcision avails anything, but faith working through love.

Any time you think that you need to *do* something in order to receive anything from God, other than believing, you are going back to the law. By doing so, you are in effect saying that what Jesus did was not good enough or what He did was not sufficient—that you have to complete the work or add something more to it.

This happened to me several times. I would say to myself, "Maybe if I fast for a week, I will feel anointed." That was the law working in me, not my spirit living in grace.

Rather, if I think according to the finished work of the cross, I will say, "Thank you Jesus for anointing me," whether I feel it or not. This does not mean you never need to fast. You fast when God tells you to, not as a ritual.

Do you want to know whether you are living under the law or under grace? If you feel guilt or condemnation in your heart, this means you are still under the law. When you live by grace, you will feel freedom in your heart.

If you do not feel confidence in your faith or in your prayers, it means you are living under the law. If you are not experiencing the love, joy, and peace God has promised, then you are under the law.

When you are under the law, know that you also live under the dominion of sin. If you are afraid of God or the devil, you are living under the law.

Feeling the conviction of your sin is different from feeling guilty and condemned. The reason you feel guilty and condemned, is because you do not believe in your heart that God loves you unconditionally. You do not trust in what His Son did for you. When you are convicted, you repent once, and keep moving. Do not stay there for another second.

I once sowed one of the largest financial seeds into someone's life that I have ever sowed. After I gave the amount, I said to myself, "Now all the generational blessings will be released into my life." But I didn't feel right in my spirit, something was wrong.

The next day the Holy Spirit told me, "You gave that money *because* you are blessed; you are not blessed because you gave that money." Right then I knew I had returned to the law. I repented and renounced that law, and thanked God for the blessing I received through Jesus Christ. Do you see the difference, my friends?

Any time you attach a condition or perform a work in order to receive something which God already promised or gave you through Christ Jesus, you are depending on either the works of the law, or your own works; and you have fallen from grace.

To fall from grace does not mean you lose your salvation. It means you are no longer free anymore, as have brought yourself back under the yoke of the law.

If one thing is conditional, then everything else is conditional. God did not give some things for free and put a price tag on others. No. He freely gave us *all* things.

Romans 8:32, He who did not spare His own Son, but delivered Him up for us all, how shall He not with Him also **freely give us all things**?

Why do we feel that God has not blessed us with some things? Why do we think certain things are conditional?

It is because in that area of our lives we are living under the law; maybe a law from the Bible, or one we made up ourselves. When you renounce that law, and exercise your faith, you can have anything you believe.

You can receive the grace of God in vain

Do you know why many people do not walk in the power of God? They believe they have to obey the law; and, as long as they believe that, the grace they received becomes void. If we could in anyway improve our lives ourselves, then there was no need for Christ to die for us.

> 2 Corinthians 6:1, We then, *as* workers together *with Him* also plead with *you* not to receive the grace of God in vain.

You can make your faith void and the promises of God ineffective

Though you have received a measure of faith from God, you can make it void, meaning it will do you no good. You will be like a person in the world who lives and walks by what they think and feel (or by sight).

> Romans 4:13-16, For the promise that he would be the heir of the world *was* not to Abraham or to his seed through the law, but through the righteousness of faith.
>
> For if those who are of the law *are* heirs, **faith is made void** and the **promise made of no effect,** because the law brings about wrath; for where there is no law *there is* no transgression.

Therefore *it is* of faith that *it might be* according to grace, so that the promise might be sure to all the seed, not only to those who are of the law, but also to those who are of the faith of Abraham, who is the father of us all.

You can frustrate the grace of God

God made you a righteous person in Christ Jesus, but when you keep going back to the law in order to become or feel righteous, you are frustrating the grace of God. You are trying to earn what God has given you for free.

The Bible says He has freely given us all things. Do not frustrate the grace of God. Repent, and accept His offer; and then, let your soul find peace and rest in Jesus' name. If you could become a good person and be accepted by God by keeping the law, then Christ died in vain.

> Galatians 2:21 (KJV), I do not frustrate the grace of God: for if righteousness come by the law, then Christ is dead in vain.

THE PURPOSE OF GIVING THE LAW

The law was given to increase the offense

The more you try to keep the law, the more you mess up; because it was given to increase the offense so that people will realize their need and cry out for a Savior.

When you get tired of trying to keep the law, tired of trying to live right and still not meeting the standard, you give up. But if you go to God, He will give you the revelation of His grace. He will say, "I never told you to try, I have done it for you, so you enter into My rest."

The whole Christian life is summed up in six words: "It is written," and, "It is finished." We need to know when to say which. Such is the wisdom we need to receive from the Spirit of God.

Some people become like monks in order to utterly try and keep the law with the utmost intensity. Such are not suited for living amongst other people; rather, only in a cave somewhere.

Jesus did not live in a cave even though He kept all the law, and fulfilled it for us. He mostly hung out with sinners, drinking and eating (Matthew 11:19).

> Romans 5:20-21, Moreover the **law entered that the offense might abound**. But where sin abounded, grace abounded much more, so that as sin reigned in death, even so grace might reign through righteousness to eternal life through Jesus Christ our Lord.

The law was given to bring us to Christ

> Galatians 3:23-25 (KJV), But before faith came, we were kept under the law, shut up unto the

faith which should afterwards be revealed. Wherefore the law was our schoolmaster to bring us unto Christ, that we might be justified by faith. But after that faith is come, we are no longer under a schoolmaster.

We all may begin with the law, the schoolmaster, when we start our walk with the Lord. But once we are in Christ and receive freedom through His Spirit, we should no longer remain under such (law), even for a day; choosing instead, to live under grace, and be led by His Spirit.

Who needs rules and regulations? Children and spiritual children need the law, not mature children and adults. Paul calls those who teach the law, instructors of babes.

Please read the following verses:

> Romans 2:20, An instructor of the foolish, a teacher of babes, having the form of knowledge and truth in the law.

> Galatians 4:1-7 (KJV), Now I say, that the heir, as long as he is a child, differeth nothing from a servant, though he be lord of all; but is under tutors and governors until the time appointed of the father.

> Even so we, when we were children, were in bondage under the elements of the world: But

> when the fullness of the time was come, God sent forth his Son, made of a woman, made under the law, **to redeem them that were under the law**, that we might receive the adoption of sons.
>
> And because ye are sons, God hath sent forth the Spirit of his Son into your hearts, crying, Abba, Father. Wherefore thou art no more a servant, but a son; and if a son, then an heir of God through Christ.

Every child needs rules and regulations because their conscience is not developed nor trained to know the difference between right and wrong. However, there comes a time when each child needs to make his or her own decisions. The sooner this happens, the better it is for the child and the parents.

We all start with the same rules, "Do not touch, do not taste, do not handle." The Bible calls these the elementary things (rudiments) of this world (Galatians 4:9-11; Colossians 2:20-23).

When you become an adult, you do the right thing not because someone forces you, but because the law is in your heart. You do not keep a set of rules in your pocket that was given by someone else so that you can take it out and read it to know good from evil. Rather, this is what God said in the Scriptures, "I will put my law and Spirit within them and cause them to walk in my ways" (Hebrews 9:8-13; 10:15-17).

> Hebrews 5:13-14, For everyone who partakes *only* of milk *is* unskilled in the word of righteousness, for he is a babe. But solid food belongs to those who are of full age, *that is,* those who by reason of use have their senses exercised to discern both good and evil.

Unfortunately, today there are many believers who have not made this transition in their lives. They are still under the tutor (rules and regulations) though they have been children of God for many years. They are spiritual babes.

It's high time to make that transition and walk in the freedom Christ has given us. When people hear of their freedom in Christ, many will only think about freedom from the Old Testament animal sacrifices or lawless living. That is not all it is talking about.

Rather, it is freedom from the spirit of bondage, and freedom to walk in the Spirit. As I said earlier, we all need the law until we receive the revelation of the love and the grace of God in our heart—which is supposed to happen when we come to Christ. For many, this takes a long time to figure out. Once we receive it, we are no longer under the law. Otherwise, no one would be able to safely live on this earth.

The law was given to show us our hopelessness

The Israelites couldn't keep the law, but not because they did not want to. They tried to, but realized there was no way they were able to fulfill all that was required. No one in the Old Testament was made righteous because they obeyed the law. Otherwise, God did not have to send Jesus to die for us. The Psalmist says, "There is none who does good, No, not one" (Psalm 14:3; 53:3).

What the law could not do because of sin, God sent His Son to fulfill, so that the righteousness of God could come upon us who believe in Christ.

> Romans 8:3-4, For what the law could not do in that it was weak through the flesh, God *did* by sending His own Son in the likeness of sinful flesh, on account of sin: He condemned sin in the flesh, that the righteous requirement of the law might be fulfilled in us who do not walk according to the flesh but according to the Spirit.

The law was given as a shadow of good things to come

> Hebrews 10:1, For the law, having a shadow of the good things to come, *and* not the very image of the things, can never with these same sacrifices, which they offer continually year by year, make those who approach perfect.

Jesus Fulfilled the Law for Us

> Matthew 5:17, Do not think that I came to destroy the Law or the Prophets. I did not come to destroy but to **fulfill**.

Besides Jesus, no human being ever fulfilled all the requirements of the law. So stop deceiving yourself by thinking that you are some spiritual superhero who can keep the law. No one did and no one can.

God knew that when He gave the law, because He wanted to let man see what was in him. Jesus fulfilled everything that was required by the law for us, so we do not need to try keeping it anymore.

According to the Old Testament, when you fulfilled the requirements of the law, all of the blessings that were promised by God would come into your life. So, because of what Jesus did, you and I are freely blessed by every blessing promised by God.

Do not let the enemy, who will tell you to keep the law, cheat you out of your blessing. Cast him out and say, "Devil, Jesus fulfilled the law for me; and all the blessings God mentioned in the Old Testament, are mine. Amen."

God Introduced a New Law

The universe and the world we live in are both governed by laws. There are natural and spiritual laws. Gravity is a natural law, while the law of aerodynamics is a law that is superior to gravity. When you apply the law of thermodynamics, cold water turns to steam.

The problem with humanity was that we were held in bondage under the law of sin and death.

God gave the Law (the Ten Commandments) to make mankind know the extent of their depravity and their inability to do anything good without Him. He knew that human beings do not admit defeat or weakness that easily. They will always find a good deed to hang onto; thinking that will make them righteous, and save them from hell.

There is a tendency in us to think that we are (our sin is) not as bad as someone else out there in the world. We try to justify ourselves through such comparisons. God wants mankind to admit their sin and ask Him for help. In truth, the law accomplished that.

> Galatians 3:23-26, But before faith came, we were kept under guard by the law, kept for the faith which would afterward be revealed.
>
> Therefore the law was our tutor *to bring us* to Christ, that we might be justified by faith. But after faith has come, we are no longer under a tutor. For you are all sons of God through faith in Christ Jesus.

For the law of sin and death (Romans 7:23, 25; 8:2) to be broken, there has to be a superior law. That law is called the law of the Spirit of life in Christ Jesus. We remained under the law of sin and death until the new law was introduced.

> Romans 8:2-4, For the law of the Spirit of life in Christ Jesus has made me free from the law of sin and death.
>
> For what the law could not do in that it was weak through the flesh, God *did* by sending His own Son in the likeness of sinful flesh, on account of sin: He condemned sin in the flesh, that the righteous requirement of the law might be fulfilled in us who do not walk according to the flesh but according to the Spirit.

God gave us new commandments

You may ask whether a Christian needs to obey any commandment at all. Yes, we do. In fact, we need to obey two commandments. Jesus gave us two new commandments.

> John 13:34, **A new commandment I give to you**, that you love one another; as I have loved you, that you also love one another.
>
> John 3:18, He who believes in Him is not condemned; but he who does not believe is

condemned already, because he has not believed in the name of the only begotten Son of God.

John 8:24, Therefore I said to you that you will die in your sins; for if you do not **believe** that I am He, you will die in your sins.

1 John 3:22-23, And whatever we ask we receive from Him, because we keep His commandments and do those things that are pleasing in His sight. **And this is His commandment:** that we should believe on the name of His Son Jesus Christ and love one another, as He gave us commandment.

1 John 5:2-3, By this we know that we love the children of God, when we love God and keep His commandments. For this is the love of God, that we keep His commandments. And His commandments are not burdensome.

According to the verses above, a believer in Christ is required to keep two commandments. These are to believe in Jesus Christ, and to love one another.

God's only requirement

There is only one way to obey the new commandment; that is to walk in the Spirit. The one and only thing God requires from us now to obey Him, is to walk in the Spirit.

When you walk in the Spirit, you will automatically fulfill all the righteous requirements of the law. You will not fulfill the lust of the flesh.

Do not follow any rules and regulations, but follow your regenerated spirit and the Holy Spirit. Those who are led by the Spirit of God are the children of God—not those who keep rules and regulations. Be free in Jesus' name!

When you walk in the Spirit you will find that the flesh, sin, the law, the devil, or the world will have no effect on you. Romans 8:13-15, "For if you live according to the flesh you will die; but if by the Spirit you put to death the deeds of the body, you will live. For as many as are led by the Spirit of God, these are sons of God. For you did not receive the spirit of bondage again to fear, but you received the Spirit of adoption by whom we cry out, 'Abba, Father.'"

We can make our own law

A law in someone's life did not necessarily come from the Bible. People make up their own laws all the time, and bring themselves under bondage. Whatever rules or regulations you apply to your life will become a law for you.

If you are thinking, "If I do this, God will be pleased with me; and if I do not do that, God will be mad at me;" or when you say you will never do or say something again, you have put yourself under a law. Sooner or later you will break that law, and feel condemned.

For example, if someone says, "I will *never* drink coffee ever again," they just put themselves under a law. After a couple of weeks, they go out to breakfast with their friends and are tempted by the smell of the coffee that was coming from their friend's cup. They give in to the temptation and take a sip. Bam! The law that they created suddenly brings the sin nature alive, and they feel guilt and condemnation.

The devil, taking occasion, begins tormenting them. "Look at you, you just broke a law; you cannot even keep one, single rule. You are worthless and now you have to be punished." As a result, we feel bad about ourselves. That whole day may be ruined until we make a new law. Life keeps going like this.

That is not the kind of life Christ came to give to us. Drinking coffee is just an example; it could be anything that pertains to life.

Our parents put so many laws into our lives. When we were growing up we heard, "You can't do that," "Don't touch that," "Never say that again," etc., etc. The Bible calls those the elementary principles (rules) of the world. They are all laws by which our mind has been programmed.

Once you come to Christ, you are free from those. However, because we have been programmed with those elementary rules from childhood, it is difficult for us to think differently.

This does not mean, however, that children are not to obey their parent's rules. The main reason that parents have rules for their children is to teach and train them how to live properly, and to keep them safe. Without that training many children would not learn important lessons in their lives or could come to great harm. The point here, is once you are grown, you are no longer to place burdens on yourself by making laws that bind your heart instead of setting you free. Once you've grown up you are not governed by your parents rules and regulations. You are expected to reach a level of maturity where you are able to exercise your own will to choose between right and wrong, and what to do and what not to do.

This is what needs to happen to every person. Until we are brought to Christ, everyone is governed by various laws, including religious laws. But after you come to Christ, you are no longer led by those laws (Galatians 3:24-25), but by the Spirit of God Who is in you. Because those who are led by the Spirit of God—not by laws—are the children of God (Romans 8: 14).

> Colossians 2:20-23, Therefore, if you died with Christ from the basic principles of the world, why, as *though* living in the world, do you subject yourselves to regulations— 'Do not touch, do not taste, do not handle,' which all concern

things which perish with the using—according to the commandments and doctrines of men?

These things indeed have an appearance of wisdom in self-imposed religion, *false* humility, and neglect of the body, *but are* of no value against the indulgence of the flesh.

Galatians 4:9-11, But now after you have known God, or rather are known by God, how *is it that* you turn again to the weak and beggarly elements, to which you desire again to be in bondage? You observe days and months and seasons and years. I am afraid for you, lest I have labored for you in vain.

People have made all sorts of laws that have nothing to do with the Bible or the law of the Spirit of life. Make sure you uproot all the laws you are keeping or have brought upon yourself, but instead throw these at the foot of the cross, never to pick them up again.

If you look at churches today they all function under laws. We are not to be led by the law, but by the Spirit. One reason why the blessings of the New Covenant are not manifesting in our lives is not because of the devil, but because we are living under laws we ourselves have made.

This is why Paul said there is nothing unclean in itself, unless to someone who thinks it is unclean. Romans

14:14, "I know and am convinced by the Lord Jesus that *there is* nothing unclean of itself; but to him who considers anything to be unclean, to him *it is* unclean."

> Romans 2:14-15, For when Gentiles, who do not have the law, by nature do the things in the law, these, **although not having the law, are a law to themselves,** who show the work of the law written in their hearts, their conscience also bearing witness, and between themselves *their* thoughts accusing or else excusing *them*.

Paul said in 1 Corinthians 6:12, "All things are lawful for me, but all things are not helpful. All things are lawful for me, but I will not be brought under the power of any."

Any time we keep a law, we kick-start the curse of the law. Whether it is one from the Bible, or one we make, those who follow the law are under a curse.

> Galatians 3:10, For as many as are of the works of the law are under the curse; for it is written, 'Cursed *is* everyone who does not continue in all things which are written in the book of the law, to do them.'

You cannot take one law and avoid the next. Either you do it all, or you do not do any at all. James 2:10, "For whoever shall keep the whole law, and yet stumble in one *point,* he is guilty of all."

CHAPTER 2

The Benefits of Grace

Now that we have learnt about the law and its purpose, let's learn about the grace of God and the benefits of living in grace.

There will be no transgression

> Romans 4:15, Because the law brings about wrath; for where there is no law *there is* no transgression.

Do you want to know the secret of living free from sin? Be free from the law. When there is no law, there is no transgression. When you are free from the law, you lose the desire to sin.

Without the law, sin is dead. It has no power because the law empowers our sin nature. The law was not given to cure sin but to bring the knowledge of sin.

Many people are afraid that if they do not keep the law, their life will get out of control, and they will go on to commit some horrible sin. The opposite is true. When you are free from the law and come under the dominion of grace, you will be free from the grip of sin; and, for the first time, you will be free to live the life God wants you to live without fear.

Romans 7:8, But sin, taking opportunity by the commandment, produced in me all *manner of evil* desire. For apart from the law sin *was* dead.

Sin is no longer a problem. The devil uses fear to keep us from knowing the truth. He does not want us to be free. If you are still bound by sin and the law, you are his illegal prisoner.

The devil has no right to keep us under his dominion because he lost his right of ownership. It was cancelled by the blood of Jesus. The whole world is free and can be free, but they do not know that yet. We must tell them this truth. Amen.

No more guilt and condemnation

> Romans 8:1, *There is* therefore now no condemnation to those who are in Christ Jesus, who do not walk according to the flesh, but according to the Spirit.

The reason we feel guilty and condemned when we do something wrong is because of the law. When you are in Christ and under grace, condemnation has no place in your heart, because you know in your heart you were accepted as the beloved of God, in spite of what you did or did not do.

Sin will not have any dominion over you

> Romans 6:14, For sin shall not have dominion over you, for you are not under law but under grace.

One of the main concerns that legalistic people have against the grace of God being taught, is that they think if we preach grace and not enough law, people will become lawless and commit sin or receive a license to sin. This is a total misconception.

As the verse above says, when you come under grace, sin loses its dominion over you; and gradually you will stop sinning altogether. On the other hand, people who are living under the law commit sin like every other person in the world. They cannot stop sin by keeping the law; instead, the law empowers sin.

You have the freedom to come into God's presence anytime and anywhere

> Hebrews 4:16, Let us therefore come boldly to the throne of grace, that we may obtain mercy and find grace to help in time of need.

As a child of God, you have the freedom to come to the presence of God, your Father, at any time and in any location. Because of what Jesus accomplished for you, God will not and cannot reject you.

We are justified by grace through faith

> Romans 3:21-24, But now the righteousness of God apart from the law is revealed, being witnessed by the Law and the Prophets, even the righteousness of God, through faith in Jesus Christ, to all and on all who believe. For there is no difference; for all have sinned and fall short of the glory of God, **being justified freely by His grace** through the redemption that is in Christ Jesus.
>
> Romans 3:28, Therefore we conclude that a man is justified by faith apart from the deeds of the law.
>
> Acts 13:38-39, Therefore let it be known to you, brethren, that through this Man is preached to you the forgiveness of sins; and by Him everyone who believes is justified from all things from which you could not be justified by the law of Moses.

If observing the law could have justified and made a person righteous before God, then God did not have to send His Son to die and endure all that pain.

We are dead to the law and free from it through Jesus Christ

Romans 7:4, Therefore, my brethren, you also have become dead to the law through the body of Christ, that you may be married to another—to Him who was raised from the dead, that we should bear fruit to God.

Romans 7:6, But **now we have been delivered from the law**, having died to what we were held by, so that we should serve in the newness of the Spirit and not *in* the oldness of the letter.

We have been redeemed from the law

Galatians 4:4-5, But when the fullness of the time had come, God sent forth His Son, born of a woman, born under the law, to redeem those who were under the law, that we might receive the adoption as sons.

Most of us are waiting for Jesus to appear in a vision, to send an angel, or even for that special anointed person to come and lay hands on us, in order to set us free. My friend, there is nothing left for Jesus to set you free from. You are free from those things you believe you are free from! It's up to you now. The choice is yours.

Jesus said, "And you shall know the truth, and the truth shall make you free" (John 8:32).

The reason we feel we are not free in some areas is because we do not yet know the truth. When you know the truth, you will experience it in your life.

Please read the chart below in order to understand the difference between the Old and the New Testament, and to see which covenant you are living under:

Old Testament / Old Covenant	New Testament / New Covenant)
If you obey, I will bless you	You are already blessed (Ephesians 1:3; 2 Peter 1:3)
The land I will give to you	All things are yours (1 Corinthians 3:21-22)
If you do not obey My voice, I will leave you to your enemies	I will never leave you nor forsake you (Hebrews 13:5)
If you sanctify yourself…	You have been made holy and blameless (Ephesians 1:4)
If you walk in My ways…	I will cause you to walk in My ways (Hebrews 8:9-11)
If you obey, I will not put any sickness on you	You are healed (1 Peter 2:24)
I will go before you and defeat your enemies	Our enemy is already defeated (Colossians 2:14-15)

If you bring the right sacrifice, I will forgive you	All sins are forgiven because of one perfect sacrifice (Hebrews 10:11-12)
If you are holy, I will dwell among you	We are the temple of His Spirit. He dwells in us (1 Corinthians 3:16; 6:19)
Some special people are anointed	Everyone is anointed (2 Corinthians 1:21)
Servants	Sons (John 1:12)
A select few are priests and kings	Each believer is a king and a priest at the same time (Royal priesthood) (1 Peter 2:9; Revelation 1:6; 5:10)
Priests need to offer the sacrifices every year	Christ offered Himself once and for all (Hebrews 9:12)
No permission to come to His presence	Come to His presence anytime boldly (Hebrews 4:16)
If you do this, based on works and keeping rules…	Based on faith and belief only (Hebrews 11:6)

Righteousness is a free gift

Again, you did not become a sinner by sinning. We all became sinners because of Adam's transgression. So, it is unfair for God's justice system to punish us.

Also, it is unrealistic for God to demand that we do everything right when He knows it is impossible for fallen human beings.

He decided to forgive our sins and make us righteous in spite of who we are and what we did:

> Romans 5:17-19, For if by the one man's offense death reigned through the one, much more those who receive abundance of grace and of the gift of righteousness will reign in life through the One, Jesus Christ.
>
> Therefore, as through one man's offense *judgment came* to all men, resulting in condemnation, even so through one Man's righteous act *the free gift came* to all men, resulting in justification of life.

For as by one man's disobedience many were made sinners, so also by one Man's obedience many will be made righteous.

You do not need to look or act pious in order to receive the free gift, because it does not depend on your behavior. It depends solely on what Jesus did on the cross.

Salvation is a gift

Just like righteousness is a free gift, salvation is a free gift. You do not need to crawl on the floor or climb any hillside in order to be saved; just believe.

> Ephesians 2:8-9, For by grace you have been saved through faith, and that not of yourselves; *it is* the gift of God, not of works, lest anyone should boast.

We are not saved by prayer or baptism, but by simple faith in Christ Jesus and what He did for us. That's it.

Everything else God gives us—is free

God gave everything to Adam for free. Genesis 2:16, "And the Lord God commanded the man, saying, 'Of every tree of the garden you may **freely** eat.'"

> Romans 8:32, He who did not spare His own Son, but delivered Him up for us all, how shall He not with Him also **freely give us all things**?

> 1 Corinthians 2:12, Now we have received, not the spirit of the world, but the Spirit who is from God, that we might know the things that have been **freely given to us by God**.

> 2 Peter 1:3, "As His divine power has given to us all things that *pertain* to life and godliness, through the knowledge of Him who called us by glory and virtue."

There is nothing we could earn from God by our good works or through keeping any law. He has already blessed us with everything we need. It was given to us as a free gift. The only thing we can do is receive it with thanksgiving.

When there is no law—sin is not imputed

> Romans 5:13, For until the law sin was in the world, but **sin is not imputed when there is no law**.

If Christ is the end of the law, and by grace we are freed from the bondage of sin and the law, then sin is no longer imputed. What does This mean?

To impute means to credit something to your account. When God says sin is not imputed, it means that when you commit a sin now, it is not credited to your life. Rather, God imputes that sin to the cross and to the blood of Jesus.

God is not walking behind you taking note of every little thing you do wrong so that He can write it down in His book. There was a time like that, but that was during the Old Covenant. Jesus nailed the writing that was against us to the cross, and removed it forever (Colossians 2:14).

Grace is not a license to sin, but the power to walk in victory. You will not sin if you walk and live in grace; believe me. But, if you try to keep the law, you will stumble, you will sin, and you will never enjoy the Christian life God has purchased for you on this earth.

I used to be afraid of sin when I was not free from the dominion of sin. I believed that if I sinned, God was going to be mad at me and take away my anointing, and that I would lose my calling or salvation.

Now I know why most believers are miserable, feel defeated, and are waiting to get out of this earth. They are being tormented by the devil for the sins and mistakes they commit because they are still living under the law.

Every time you transgress a law, there is punishment. But, if you are in Christ, you are not under the law, but are free from the dominion of sin. There is no transgression or condemnation.

The devil has no right to make you feel condemned. You need to rebuke and renounce this any time you feel condemned. You have passed from judgment to life.

If you look at the life of Abraham, the father of our faith, you will learn how to live the Christian life.

He was the first person to whom the gospel was preached (Galatians 3:8). He was the first individual who lived under grace. Abraham was not a perfect man. He committed many sins in his life, but we do not see God punishing him for them.

Is God partial? Was Abraham God's favorite? No. However, he understood something about God that very few people discover in their lifetime.

Abraham saw the day of Jesus on this earth and lived in it, by faith, thousands of years before Jesus' coming (John 8:56). He saw the day when God forgives people's sin not based on their goodness but on His love. He believed it, and God accounted that to him for righteousness.

When God told Abraham to leave his country and his father's house, he took his nephew, Lot, and his father. That was his first mistake.

He lied twice about his wife, but God rescued him (and his wife) anyway. He slept with Hagar, trying to produce the seed of the promise. God did not punish him for it. Why?

First of all, he was not under the law. The law was not yet given. Remember, when you are not under the law, sin is not imputed.

Secondly, he was living under the grace of God. God was showing us through Abraham what it means to live in the age of grace. Man has the freedom to live under the law or grace. It is our choice.

What would you do if you did not feel condemned? How different would you feel if you knew that God had forgiven all your sins and that He does not keep a record of wrongs? What would you do if you knew that God loves you unconditionally, not based on your works? Would you have more confidence toward God? Would you share that love with more people? Yes, of course.

Or, would you feel like sinning more? I don't think so. You are loved, you are forgiven, and you have victory over sin and the devil. If you truly know you are forgiven, you will love God all the more (Luke 7:46-48). Get up now and dance!

It is not easy to live in the grace of God. Though it is a free gift, we have a natural tendency to go back to the law. As fallen humans we like rules and regulations, we like the feeling of being in control.

Remember, man chose the way of good and evil in the beginning, which was a foreshadowing of the law. Adam tried to be like God based on his own merits. Knowingly or unknowingly, we try to make the free gift of God conditional.

Despite the Israelites being freed from Egyptian slavery, when things did not seem to go the way they thought they should, their first tendency was to go back to Egypt. Though they knew it was slavery, they found out that it was harder to live free trusting in God, than living in bondage.

As long as we live on this earth, there will be a tendency in us to go back to the law (bondage). We need to examine ourselves to see whether we are in faith.

> 2 Corinthians 13:5, Examine yourselves *as to* whether you are in the faith. Test yourselves. Do you not know yourselves, that Jesus Christ is in you?—unless indeed you are disqualified.

We need to grow in the grace of God. "You therefore, beloved, since you know *this* beforehand, beware lest you also fall from your own steadfastness, being led away with the error of the wicked; but **grow in the grace and knowledge of our Lord and Savior Jesus Christ**" (2 Peter 3:17-18). May the Lord help us all.

In the New Testament everything God does is by His grace and through our faith. The Bible says there are different levels of grace we can receive. Everyone does not receive the same amount. It's like faith. Everyone does not have the same amount of faith.

CHAPTER 3

7 Dimensions of God's Grace

God's grace comprises some seven dimensions, beginning with the following:

1. Grace for Grace

Let's look again at John 1:16.

> And of His fullness **we have all received, and grace for grace.**

This verse says that out of His fullness we all have received grace for grace. At first it confused me when I read it. I wondered what *grace for grace* meant.

It is also important to notice the phrase "**all have received.**" It was not a select few, not the most religious or holy person, not someone who belongs to a particular denomination or race. No, it means the entire human race received the grace of God.

Notwithstanding, not all are benefiting from it, mostly because they don't know that they have received this grace. They are trying to earn it by their own efforts.

God is not partial. He made His grace available to the entire human race. So, if you have any religious mindset that makes you feel you are special or superior because of your race or skin color, let's change that right now before we go any further; because this grace will not benefit you if you have such an attitude.

Now, what does *grace for grace* mean? Those two words *grace* mentioned are actually two types of grace.

The first type of grace qualifies us to receive the second type of grace. The first type of grace is the *dispensation*, or the *age* of grace that we are living in right now, which began with the coming of Jesus.

The second type of grace is the grace that we receive according to our need and the measure of Christ, because we live in the age of grace. Without the first we cannot access the second.

> John 1:17, For the law was given through Moses, *but* **grace** and truth came through Jesus Christ.

First of all, you need to make sure you are living in the age of grace. You are not under the law or any customs of the Old Testament. If you are, you will not be able to receive the grace of God.

Even if there is a slight sense of self-righteousness or a tendency to depend on the law or your own works, this grace will not benefit you.

> Romans 10:4, For **Christ** is the end of the law for righteousness to everyone who believes.

Christ did not come to add a comma to the law, but to put an end to it. He did not come to continue or add things to the law, but to fulfill it; and make the old covenant obsolete (Hebrews 8:10-13).

He did not say on the cross, "To be continued," but He said, "It is finished." That meant Jesus fulfilled everything God required of us, on our behalf. He is the only person on this earth who fulfilled the entire law. Not one single human being could meet all that was required of the Old Testament laws.

> Romans 6:14, For sin shall not have dominion over you, for you are not under law but under grace.

If sin has any dominion over you, you are not under the grace of God yet, but still under the law. As I said before, everything works according to a law. Grace is a law. When you operate under this law, sin cannot have any dominion over you. It's impossible.

It's like when you fly in an airplane, the law of gravity has no influence on you because that airplane is operating on a law that is superior to the law of gravity, called aerodynamics. As long as that airplane flies at a certain speed, gravity cannot bring it down. However, if it slows down enough, gravity begins to have its pull.

One of the problems in the Body of Christ is that many realize that they live in the age of grace, but knowingly or unknowingly, they tend to go back to the Old Testament.

Human beings like to do something to earn something. Many people do not like to receive something for free. Because of their ego or pride they would rather pay or work to deserve or earn something because it makes them feel better about themselves.

This mentality will not work when it comes to the grace of God. If it could have been earned, the richest man on this earth or the most religiously afflicted soul might deserve it more than us. But thank God, He is not dealing with us based on our merits.

How do we access this grace that is made available to us? The age of grace means God deals with man not based on our personal merits, but based on the abundance of His love, mercy, kindness, forgiveness, blessings, and power.

> Romans 5:2, Through whom also we have **access by faith into this grace** in which we stand, and rejoice in hope of the glory of God.

It is by faith we access this grace. There is one thing that pleases God, and that is faith. The Bible says that without faith it is impossible to please Him (Hebrews 11:6).

2. Salvation Grace

> Titus 2:11, For the **grace of God** that brings salvation has appeared to all men.

In the fullness of time God sent His Son, born of a virgin, to save all mankind. It is the grace of God that brings salvation to all men.

The verse above says that grace has appeared to all men. God has extended the grace for salvation to all men—meaning the entire human race. However, many do not receive it because of ignorance and spiritual blindness.

> Ephesians 2:4-9, But God, who is rich in mercy, because of His great love with which He loved us, even when we were dead in trespasses, made us alive together with Christ (by grace you have been saved), and raised *us* up together, and made *us* sit together in the heavenly *places* in Christ Jesus, that in the ages to come He might show the exceeding riches of His grace in *His* kindness toward us in Christ Jesus. **For by grace you have been saved through faith, and that not of yourselves; it**

is the gift of God, not of works, lest anyone should boast.

The verse above says that God, Who is rich in mercy, and because of His great love by which He loved us, decided to show the exceeding riches of His grace in His kindness.

I hope you can recall the definition of grace. It is His love, favor, mercy, kindness, compassion, forgiveness, blessings, and power bestowed upon us. The verses above describe all of these, in one way or other.

Salvation is a gift from God to us. We don't deserve it, nor do we earn it by doing something. This is a hard concept for us to grasp, because we have a tendency to think it depends on us doing something.

Rather, it is based on what Jesus did for us on the cross. Many live in fear of losing their salvation and not keeping some law from the Old Testament or some Jewish traditions.

> Luke 1:74-75, To grant us that we, being delivered from the hand of our enemies, might serve Him without fear, in holiness and righteousness before Him all the days of our life.

The Old Testament was based on fear, and was called the ministry of death (2 Corinthians 3:7).

Every great king and every great nation likes to display their military power and wealth. Countries have military parades and practices in different regions to show off their power to other nations. This is exactly what God did toward us. He demonstrated the exceeding greatness of His love, mercy, kindness, compassion, forgiveness, blessings, and power to us.

> 2 Timothy 1:9, Who has saved us and called *us* with a holy calling, not according to our works, but according to His own purpose and grace which was given to us in Christ Jesus before time began.

3. Grace for Gifts

> Romans 12:6-8, Having then **gifts differing according to the grace** that is given to us, *let us use them:* if prophecy, *let us prophesy* in proportion to our faith; or ministry, *let us use it* in *our* ministering; he who teaches, in teaching; he who exhorts, in exhortation; he who gives, with liberality; he who leads, with diligence; he who shows mercy, with cheerfulness.

Each believer in Christ has received a gift from God at the time of his or her salvation. You have received it according to the measure of Christ's gift.

> Ephesians 4:7, But to **each one of us grace was given** according to the measure of Christ's gift.

What is the measure of Christ's gift? How does He measure when He gives gifts to someone? What standard does He use?

An example I like, is a story about Alexander the Great:

> When he became great, one of his childhood friends came to see him with a special request. This friend was very poor compared to Alexander, and the king was very happy to see his old friend.
>
> When Alexander asked him what he could do for him, his friend requested the king give a small house, for him and his family. Alexander replied that when he gives gifts, he gives according to his capacity and not according to the needs of the person.
>
> Instead of giving his friend a small house, the king appointed him as the governor of a new territory he had conquered.

Wow! That is a great story.

When Christ measures to give something to someone, He does not just give according to our needs, but according to His capacity. As we read in the verses above, the riches of His grace and glory have no limit.

The measure that He measures is more than enough for what we need. This is why the Bible says in Ephesians 3:20, "Now to Him who is able to do exceedingly abundantly above all that we ask or think, according to the power that works in us."

What is the purpose of the gift God gave us?

It is to minister to one another. There is someone in your sphere of influence who is in need of your gift, whether it is a believer or your unsaved neighbor.

When you use your gift to minister to others, they get blessed, and in turn they will be touched by God, and He will bless you.

> 1 Peter 4:10, As each one has received a gift, minister it to one another, as good stewards of the manifold grace of God.

There is not a single believer who has not received a gift. You may not have discovered it yet. The more you use your gift(s) the better you become at it.

Discover your gifts as early as possible, and use them, and you will be blessed more and more as the days go by.

No one can say they have not received anything, or what they have is not important or insignificant. Remember the parable of the talents. Everyone received talents according to his ability and capacity.

4. Grace to Give

> 2 Corinthians 8:1-2, Moreover, brethren, we make known to you the grace of God bestowed on the churches of Macedonia: that in a great trial of affliction the abundance of their joy and

their deep poverty abounded in the riches of their liberality.

The churches in Macedonia were not rich churches, meaning the believers were comparatively poorer than the believers in Corinth. Paul was saying the churches in Macedonia received the grace of God to give in spite of their deep poverty. He was telling the Corinthian church to follow their example.

> 2 Corinthians 8:6-7, So we urged Titus, that as he had begun, so he would also complete this grace in you as well. But as you abound in everything—in faith, in speech, in knowledge, in all diligence, and in your love for us— *see* that you abound **in this grace also**.

Paul is saying the Corinthian Church needs to *abound in this grace also.* Which grace is he talking about? The grace to give.

Though the Corinthian church was blessed spiritually and financially, they were a stingy church. They did not have the grace to give.

Why do we need to give? Unless we give, we will never receive financial breakthrough. Many people remain at the same financial level for many years, never having enough and always struggling to meet their needs.

That is not the kind of life God wants us to live. He wants to us to have more than enough to share with others.

There is a grace that is available from God to give. When you give, you will receive.

Many people living in the New Covenant still hold on to the principle of the tithe. A tithe is ten percent of your income that you give to God.

However, in the New Testament, Jesus did not set the limit of giving to ten percent. He took the limits off, and allows each person to decide how much he or she wants to give, and how much they want to receive back.

> Luke 6:38, Give, and it will be given to you: good measure, pressed down, shaken together, and running over will be put into your bosom. **For with the same measure that you use, it will be measured back to you.**

The above verse is the standard for giving in the New Testament. The same measure that we use will be measured back to us. This means that if we give ten percent a multiplication of ten will be measured back to us. If we give five percent a multiplication of five will be measured back to us.

I pray that you receive this grace and go to the next level in your financial life. Each season God will come and require something from you to give by faith.

As I mentioned before, everything God does in the New Testament is by His grace and through our faith.

It will take all your faith to obey Him. Your obedience determines whether or not you will go to the next level.

Paul teaches the same principle in his epistles. 2 Corinthians 9:6-7, "But this *I say*: He who sows sparingly will also reap sparingly, and he who sows bountifully will also reap bountifully. *So let* each one *give* as he purposes in his heart, not grudgingly or of necessity; for God loves a cheerful giver."

5. Grace for Finances

> 2 Corinthians 8:9, For you know the **grace of our Lord Jesus Christ**, that though He was rich, yet for your sakes He became poor, that you through His poverty might become rich.

There is a grace of God that is available to meet all your financial needs. The reason Jesus became poor and was born in a manger was for our sake. The Philippian church was poor, but generous, and they were supportive of Paul's ministry. In turn, Paul said that God would meet all their needs according to His riches in glory in Christ Jesus (Philippians 4:19).

Your financial provision is attached to your purpose. God is committed to your purpose. He created you with a very specific reason in mind, and gifted you with everything you need to fulfill that purpose. You may not be aware of it yet.

You can be a receptionist in an office, and that could be your purpose. Purpose gives you fulfillment. When I preach and minister, it gives me fulfillment. The happiest time for me is after I preach under the anointing. There is such love, peace, and joy that fills my heart; and I feel totally satisfied. If I don't minister for a while then I feel irritated and dissatisfied.

There is not a person in the Bible who God called to do something and they did not have the money to do it. There is no such thing in the Bible. So, the notion some people have that if they had more money they could have done what God wanted them, to do is absolutely wrong thinking.

All you need, is to receive the grace of God. How do we receive the grace of God? By faith, just like we receive salvation. You believe in your heart and confess with your mouth.

> 2 Corinthians 9:8, And **God** is able to make all grace abound toward you, that you, always having all sufficiency in all *things,* may have an abundance for every good work.

The verse above is a very important verse in this study guide. This is the state God wants all His children to operate from. When it says "all grace," it means there is more than one type of grace.

We must receive all of His grace so that we always have all sufficiency in all things, and have an abundance for every good work. Please memorize the verse above, and keep speaking it whenever you can. You will see things change in your financial situation. You will move from lack to plenty, from scarcity to abundance, from not having enough to always having plenty and some left over to share.

6. The Grace to Overcome

There are many who feel stuck in their lives, with various struggles. They think that if God would just come through for them in that *one* area, they will be free to do what He wants them to do.

If you have been fighting a particular battle for a long time, and it seems there is no victory, and you prayed and asked God to give you a breakthrough for many years; it may be that God wants you to overcome it instead of delivering you from it, and do what He calls you to do in spite of it.

The change that you want, may not happen on the outside or to your circumstances; however, the struggle that you are facing, may have been sent to change you internally. What you need is a different perspective on the issue, and the grace of God will enable you to receive that perspective and triumph over it.

When Jesus asked the Father to take away the cross, the Father gave Him the grace to endure it instead of taking it away.

I hope you understand what I am trying to communicate. There are circumstances and areas in our lives that may not change as fast as we hope. In that case there is a grace of God that you can tap into, in order to overcome and live victorious.

The Apostle Paul had a situation in his life that he had to depend on the grace of God to overcome. He asked the Lord to remove it three times. I am glad he understood and heard from God after asking those three times.

Many of us keep asking God for years, and waste our precious time and life thinking He may still answer. God's ears are not deaf that He cannot hear us. I believe the problem is we don't hear when He speaks.

Paul was a mighty apostle of Jesus, but he had something he struggled with personally in his life. I am not talking about sin or sickness here.

Most individuals have something they privately struggle with which they don't open up about or share with others. It could be something that happened to you, something you did, a struggling relationship, an emotional condition, or it could be any ongoing struggle that you just cannot ignore. It keeps coming back, and it seems debilitating.

I want to encourage you that there is a grace of God which is available just for that. Ask the Lord to empower you with that grace so you can soar above that storm.

Every problem you face has a solution. What we think the solution should be, may be different from what God thinks the solution should be. It's all about perspective. Instead of solving or delivering me from some of the biggest problems that I faced, God gave me a different perspective, and Boom! The problem was solved.

If you have a problem that you have been dealing with for years, you may just need a heavenly perspective of the situation. You don't have to be a slave or a victim to that situation anymore.

> 2 Corinthians 12:7-10, And lest I should be exalted above measure by the abundance of the revelations, a thorn in the flesh was given to me, a messenger of Satan to buffet me, lest I be exalted above measure.
>
> Concerning this thing I pleaded with the Lord three times that it might depart from me. And He said to me, **'My grace is sufficient for you, for My strength is made perfect in weakness.'**
>
> Therefore most gladly I will rather boast in my infirmities, that the power of Christ may rest upon me. Therefore I take pleasure in infirmities, in reproaches, in needs, in persecutions, in distresses, for Christ's sake. For when I am weak, then I am strong.

When Paul prayed and asked God for a solution (to remove the thorn from his flesh), God said He was not going to remove it, but give the grace to overcome it; and never to let it victimize Paul again. From that moment, Paul received the grace of God, and he fulfilled his purpose and ran his race.

Many think the thorn in Paul's flesh was a sickness. I don't believe that's true because Jesus will never put on you something that He died and paid the price for on the cross. Sickness is one of those.

What Paul had in his life was persecution, infirmities, reproaches, needs, and distresses. Paul said it was a messenger of Satan sent to buffet him. All those things mentioned above are from the devil. The origin of those things are from Satan himself, including persecution. Paul did not die of any sickness and there is no evidence in the Bible that says his ministry was inconvenienced because of sickness.

God wants you to receive the grace to overcome right now as you are reading this study guide. It may be loneliness, challenges in relationships, or anything that you feel has been afflicting you. If God has not answered your prayers for a very long time, it may be that He wants you to receive His grace to live through it, instead of waiting and wasting your life.

7. Grace for Help

Do you need help with what God has called you to do? Do you have unmet needs in your life? It doesn't matter what type it is, there is a grace to meet those needs!

Hebrews 4:16, Let us therefore come boldly to the throne of grace, that we may obtain mercy and find grace to help in time of need.

God's throne is called the throne of grace. He says that any time you need help with any thing, to come boldly to the throne of His grace in order to obtain mercy, and find grace to help you in your time of need. There is a grace that is big enough to meet every need you have in your life.

Do you recall I said in the beginning of this study that this teaching will help meet all your needs? This is why! All you need to do is ask Him for the grace for the particular need that you have.

Healing comes through His grace. Say it with your mouth, "I receive the grace of God for healing in my body." Keep doing that for each area of your life. If you need a house, say, "I receive the grace of God for a house."

God is faithful and just. He will answer you speedily.

CHAPTER 4

Three Levels of Grace

There are various levels of grace that a person can receive. Though Christ's measure is more than what we need, it will not all appear at the same time. It depends on how much we trust in Him and His grace.

1. Great grace

> Acts 4:33, And with great power the apostles gave witness to the resurrection of the Lord Jesus. And **great grace** was upon them all.

There is great grace, like great faith, that Jesus mentioned in the gospels. That means in the early Church, everyone received great grace, and there was no one who had need of anything. Everyone's needs were met (Acts 4:34-35).

2. Exceeding grace

2 Corinthians 9:14-15, And by their prayer for you, who long for you because of the **exceeding grace of God** in you. Thanks *be* to God for His indescribable gift!

The church of Corinth had the exceeding grace of God. There was no lack of spiritual gifts, revelation, faith, or great miracles. God wants to release that exceeding grace upon us, His Church.

3. Abundance of grace

Romans 5:17, If by the one man's offense death reigned through the one, much more those who receive **abundance of grace** and of the gift of righteousness will reign in life through the One, Jesus Christ.

This grace has to do with our salvation. God wants you to have all His grace, His great, exceeding, and abundant grace. Receive this now by faith, in Jesus' name.

We Can Grow in the Grace of God

2 Peter 3:17-18, You therefore, beloved, since you know *this* beforehand, beware lest you also fall from your own steadfastness, being led away with the error of the wicked; but **grow in the grace** and knowledge of our Lord and

> Savior Jesus Christ. To Him *be* the glory both now and forever. Amen.

That is good news to me. I want to grow in the grace of God. In order to grow in the grace of God we need to increase in the knowledge of God. The more knowledge we have of God the more grace will operate in our life.

> 2 Peter 1:2, "Grace and peace be multiplied to you in the knowledge of God and of Jesus our Lord.

The more we increase in the true knowledge of God, the more grace and peace we will experience in our lives.

We Can Misuse the Grace of God

> Jude 4, For certain men have crept in unnoticed, who long ago were marked out for this condemnation, ungodly men, who turn the grace of our God into lewdness and deny the only Lord God and our Lord Jesus Christ.

This is happening a lot in our day and age. People misuse the grace of God for their own lusts and to gratify their flesh. They say that there is no judgment for wrong-doing, God does not judge sin anymore, and that Christians no longer need to repent of their sins, etc.

What the enemy is trying to do with such teaching is steal your reward in heaven. When you read the epistles of Paul, almost every page has a reference exhorting believers to live right or face consequences, both here and in eternity. Paul never preached cheap grace.

In the messages to the seven churches in the book of Revelation, Jesus warns those churches about the consequences of their wrong living. I think some of today's preachers don't read those verses or chapters.

Who Can Receive the Grace of God?

Now the final question is: Who can receive the grace of God? There is only one condition that God sets for anyone to receive His grace. That is the humility to receive it.

As I said earlier, many people do not like to receive anything for free. It hurts their pride and ego. In order to receive the grace of God, you need to get rid of every form of pride: racial, educational, lineage, and the pride of life that comes through accomplishments.

> James 4:6, But He gives more grace. Therefore He says: "God resists the proud, **but gives grace to the humble.**
>
> 1 Peter 5:5-6, Likewise you younger people, submit yourselves to *your* elders. Yes, all of *you* be submissive to one another, and be clothed with humility, for 'God resists the proud, but gives grace to the humble.' Therefore humble yourselves under the mighty hand of God, that He may exalt you in due time.

Let the grace of God labor for you. We have been striving for too long and not producing much. Let's join the Apostle Paul and have the grace of God do things for us with much ease.

Let the Grace of God Labor for You

> 1 Corinthians 15:10, But by the grace of God I am what I am, and His grace toward me was not in vain; but I labored more abundantly than they all, yet not I, but the grace of God *which was* with me."

Grace was such an important part of his message that Paul's epistles both start and end by a greeting with the grace of God.

> 2 Corinthians 13:14, The **grace** of the Lord Jesus Christ, and the love of God, and the communion of the Holy Spirit *be* with you all. Amen.

Kingdom First—then Grace

> Therefore, since we are receiving a kingdom which cannot be shaken, let us have grace…

Many go after the teaching of grace these days. The trouble is, that before we can gain it, we must first have a revelation of the kingdom of God.

The verse above says we will have grace *after* we receive a kingdom that cannot be shaken, because grace is the operating system of the kingdom of God. In His kingdom, God deals with us through His grace.

In computer terms, the kingdom is the *hardware,* and grace is the *software.* What good is having the most powerful software in the world with no hardware to operate it? How does that benefit anyone?

Every nation has a political or governing system. India is democratic, while China is communistic in its government. The kingdom of God is a nation ruled by a King Who is God, and He uses grace as His governing system.

Before we go after grace, we need to discover His kingdom. That is why Jesus commanded, "Seek *first* the kingdom…" (Matthew 6:33); and not grace.

I strongly recommend you go to the website of this ministry and order the book, *Kingdom Secrets to Worry Free Living.* I can promise you that would be best investment you will ever make toward your spiritual growth.

I hope this book has been a blessing to you. If you need more copies of this, please don't hesitate to call us, and we will send these to you.

If the Holy Spirit tells you to become a prayer or financial partner with this ministry, we want to present you with an opportunity to do so. Please use the contact address on the next page. Thank you so much, and may the Lord increase you more and more!

Questions

Use additional paper as needed.

1. What is the definition of the grace of God?

_____

_____

_____

_____

2. How do you know whether you are living in the age of grace?

_____

_____

_____

_____

3. Describe the experience of your salvation, and what revelation you received about it at that time.

_____

_____

_____

_____

4. List 5 differences between law and grace:

   1. _____
   2. _____
   3. _____
   4. _____
   5. _____

5. Which dimensions of the grace of God do you need right now?

   _____
   _____
   _____
   _____
   _____

6. Is there any battle that you have been facing which seems to have no victory, where you need the grace of God to overcome it? Please describe.

   _____
   _____
   _____
   _____
   _____

What are the gifts you received through the grace of God?

_____

_____

_____

_____

More Books & Resources

DISCIPLING NATIONS SERIES

Kingdom Mandate (for any donation)

Discovering the Lost Kingdom (Volume 1) $14.00

Purpose, Calling, and Gifts (Volume 2) $15.00

God's Original Design (Volume 3) $20.00

Seeing, Entering, and Manifesting the Kingdom of God (Volume 4) $20.00

The Ekklesia (Volume 5) $30.00

The Gospel of the Kingdom (Volume 6) $20.00

Power and Authority of the Church (Volume 7) $15.00

Kingdom Family (Volume 8) $15.00

The Birthing of a Kingdom Nation (Volume 9) $20.00

What Happened to God? (Volume 10) $20.00

7 Dimensions and Operations of the Kingdom of God (Volume 11) $15.00

Kingdom Economy (Volume 12) $15.00

Kingdom Government (Volume 13) $15.00

Releasing Kings and Queens to their Original Intent (Volume 14) $10.00

Kingdom Secrets to Restoring Nations Back to God (Volume 15) $20.00

Keys to Fulfilling Your Kingdom Assignment (Volume 16) $15.00

KINGDOM LIVING SERIES

The Three Most Important Decisions of Your Life $15.00

Recognizing God's Timing for Your Life $12.00
Overcoming the Spirit of Poverty $10.00
Seven Kinds of Believers $10.00
7 Dimensions of God's Glory $5.00
7 Dimensions of God's Grace $10.00
7 Kinds of Faith $7.00

HEALING OF THE NATIONS SERIES

Principles of Self Governance $20.00

KINGDOM BOOKS FOR KIDS

Genesis 126 Three Volume Book set for boys $25.00
Genesis 126 Three Volume Book set for boys $25.00
Genesis 126 Coloring Books for Boys $15.00
Genesis 126 Coloring Books for Girls $15.00

GENESIS 126 TEACHER'S MANUAL

Level 1 6-8 years $15.00
Level 2 8-10 years $15.00
Level 3 10-12 years $15.00

TO PLACE AN ORDER:

www.TheKingdomNetwork.org
Phone: 1-800-558-5020
Email: info@TheKingdomNetwork.org

Are you struggling to discover your **PURPOSE ?**
You are not supposed to fit in but stand out !

Sign up today for the
FREE Online Kingdom Course

DISCOVERING
THE LOST KINGDOM

In this course you'll DISCOVER:

>> Your true identity and purpose
>> What God is doing on the earth and how you can partner with Him in it
>> Why God created the earth and put us on this planet
>> And much more ...

FREE BOOK AND STUDY GUIDE

Why are people becoming more and more disinterested in **church and religion** globally?
Join the course, and discover
what your soul has been searching for all along.

Other courses available
>> DISCOVERING PURPOSE, CALLING AND GIFTS
>> SEEING, ENTERING AND MANIFESTING THE KINGDOM
>> GOD'S ORIGINAL DESIGN
>> The Ekklesia
>> The Next move of GOD
   And more ...

Register Now @ **www.TheKingdomUniversity.org**

Welcome to
KINGDOM DELIVERANCE
— WORKSHOP —

**Are you tired of waiting and looking for breakthroughs?
Kingdom of God has the answer.**

This kingdom deconstruct workshop is divided into EIGHT major categories which deal with the seven major areas of our life. Each one is connected to the next, and so if one of these areas dysfunctions, it will affect all other areas of your life.

1. Relationship with the Father
2. Spiritual Healing
3. Emotional Healing
4. Recognizing Purpose and Calling
5. Identifying and Mastering Natural and Spiritual Gifts
6. Finances—Learning to Live in Kingdom Economy
7. Healing Relationships
8. Physical Health

*Take action now.
Order all 8 workshop manuals today !*

Thank you so much for taking the courses from The Kingdom University. Taking a course is only the first step. We are pleased to present you with the next step—that of going through the process to get rid of all the extra weights that have been slowing and hindering you from fully living out your kingdom assignment.

Call 1 800 558 5020   www.TheKingdomNetwork.org

www.ingramcontent.com/pod-product-compliance
Lightning Source LLC
Chambersburg PA
CBHW050040080526
44586CB00014B/1388